OFF-LOOM WEAVING

LITTLE
CRAFT BOOK
SERIES

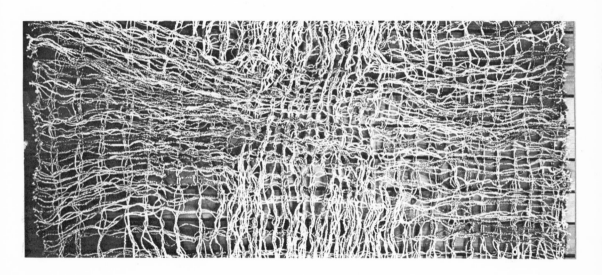

By Marion H. Bernstein

Diagrams by Susan Henderson

STERLING
PUBLISHING CO., INC.   NEW YORK

SAUNDERS OF TORONTO, Ltd., Don Mills, Canada

Oak Tree Press Co., Ltd.
London & Sydney

Little Craft Book Series

Beads Plus Macramé
Big-Knot Macramé
Candle-Making
Coloring Papers
Corrugated Carton Crafting
Creating with Beads
Creating with Burlap
Creating with Flexible Foam
Enamel without Heat
Felt Crafting
Flower Pressing
Macramé
Making Paper Flowers

Masks
Metal and Wire Sculpture
Model Boat Building
Nail Sculpture
Needlepoint Simplified
Off-Loom Weaving
Potato Printing
Puppet-Making
Repoussage
Scissorscraft
Sewing without a Pattern
Tole Painting
Whittling and Wood Carving

With love to Lennie and Zaida

Picture Credits

Rug on page 3 woven by Dorothy Dodge. Eight harness straight draw threading with off-loom appearance.

Collar on page 6 woven by Alice Marcoux.   Drawing on page 39 by Jeanne Kiefer.

The photographs on the following pages are reproduced with the courtesy of the Peabody Museum in Cambridge, Massachusetts: 16, 27, 37, 44, 46.

The photographs on the following pages are reproduced with the courtesy of the American Crafts Council, New York, New York: 29 (by Ed Rossbach), 40 (by Hal Painter), 42 (by Ed Rossbach).

The photographs on the following pages were taken by Paul Rousseff: 25, 32, 35.

Copyright © 1971 by Sterling Publishing Co., Inc.
419 Park Avenue South, New York, N.Y. 10016
Simultaneously published and Copyright © 1971 in Canada
by Saunders of Toronto, Ltd., Don Mills, Ontario
British edition published by Oak Tree Press Co., Ltd., Nassau, Bahamas
Distributed in Australia by Oak Tree Press Co., Ltd.,
P.O. Box 34, Brickfield Hill, Sydney 2000, N.S.W.
Distributed in the United Kingdom and elsewhere in the British Commonwealth
by Ward Lock Ltd., 116 Baker Street, London W 1
Manufactured in the United States of America
All rights reserved
Library of Congress Catalog Card No.: 79-167667
ISBN 0-8069-5172-9   UK 7061 2318 2
5173-7

This colorful hanging is an example of undulating fill. The technique is explained and illustrated on page 31.

Contents

Before You Begin

Weaving is one of the most natural crafts. It is enjoyable and easy to do: your hands instinctively weave, interlacing the horizontal *fill* threads into the vertical *warp* threads. People of all ages, both men and women, can create woven fabrics or articles with only a few instructions. If you have ever braided a pigtail, sewn the running stitch, darned a sock or even played checkers, then you already know how easy weaving is, because you have already woven.

Although the terms "weaving" and "clothing" are related in the minds of most people, apparel is not the only thing made by weaving. You can make dolls and handbags, lamp shades and hammocks, pillow covers and muffs by weaving. And you do not need cumbersome, expensive looms to make them. Off-loom weaving eliminates equipment that requires a whole room and a month's budget, and substitutes small, available equipment such as picture frames, ice cream sticks, or your own body. The weaving strands, like everything else in off-loom weaving, do not have to be expensive for good results. Wool left over from knitting, cloth scraps cut into strips, colored telephone cables, reeds from a pond, or a willow tree's young branches are some examples of materials to weave.

The thrill of making something from "scratch" can never be equalled. And the unique, hand-woven articles that you make with your own striking designs are sure to be valued by whoever owns them—yourself or the one who receives your thoughtful gift.

Collar

A woven collar is like jewelry: it perks up your clothing by adding new colors and textures to a plain neckline. Collars are good beginning projects, as they are easy and quick to weave.

With a tape measure, loosely measure the circumference of your neck. Draw a circle of the same circumference on a double thickness of newspaper, and draw a second circle with the same midpoint as the first, but with a radius at least 5″ larger. You can sketch this by measuring and marking 5″ from every point on the outer edge of the first circle, or use a compass for greater accuracy.

The first circle represents the edge of the collar that lies against your neck, while the outer circle is the bottom edge of the collar. Connect the neckline and bottom edge by drawing two diagonal lines that start at the same point on the neckline, but reach the bottom edge 4″ apart.

Cut the collar pattern out of the newspaper and try it on in front of a mirror, adjusting it if necessary by pinning and cutting. Trace this fitted newspaper pattern on a piece of stiff cardboard, and make small pencil marks along the neckline edge on the cardboard every $\frac{1}{8}$″. Place a ruler from the midpoint of the circles through one of the marks on the neckline edge. Then make a mark on the bottom edge of the collar when the ruler crosses it. Continue to mark the entire outer edge by placing the ruler through the midpoint and every neckline mark to find points on the bottom edge corresponding to those on the neckline.

Trace lightly around both circles of the collar with a single-edge razor blade or knife in a holder.

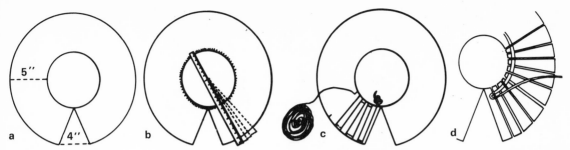

Illus. 1. In **a**, pattern to cut from cardboard for woven collar. In **b**, ruler helps mark notches along outside edge of pattern. In **c**, warp is wrapped along top of pattern. In **d**, fill goes over and under warp threads.

Go over this outline with the blade several times, scoring deeper and deeper each time until you have cut through the cardboard's entire thickness. Then use the blade to make notches $\frac{1}{4}''$ long on every point which you just marked on both collar edges.

Now that you have prepared the pattern, you are ready to fasten the warp threads around it. Tie a knot at the end of a piece of yarn and catch it on the underside in the first notch of the neckline edge. Bring the yarn across the top of the cardboard to the first notch on the bottom edge and slide the yarn into this notch. Carry the yarn along the back of the collar to the second notch of the bottom edge; then bring the yarn back up to the top side in this second notch. Take the yarn across the top of the cardboard to the second notch of the neckline edge, slide it in the notch, and carry it along the back side to the third notch of the neckline edge. Continue wrapping the yarn back and forth between the notches of both edges *on the top of the cardboard*. If you wrap the cardboard up in the yarn by simply winding the warp threads around and around the pattern, you will not be able to remove the cardboard when you are finished weaving.

After you have attached the warp threads so they are uniformly taut, begin weaving the *fill*, or weft threads. Using a needle or safety pin, thread or knot a different yarn and begin to weave it over and under every other warp thread—that is, over one thread and under the next. This basic weave is called the *tabby* weave. Leave several inches of the fill thread hanging at the starting point. When you have woven one row of fill, use a comb or fork to *beat* the yarn into place close to the neckline edge.

Weave five rows with this simple tabby weave. As you reach the end of one row, turn the thread around the end warp thread, so that if you went under that thread in the previous row, you go over it in the next row. If you run out of yarn in the middle of a row, overlap a new piece of yarn on top of the old. When you beat that row to the edge, be careful to treat the ends together so they do not separate. Never knot the yarn in weaving. If you run out of fill at the end of a row (called a *selvage*), weave a new piece of fill into the warp

Illus. 2. A woven collar using many colors and techniques. Beads have been strung on fill, and warp wrapping was used also. See page 21 for warp wrapping instructions.

the same way you began the first row, leaving a tail a few inches long. When you finish your weaving, thread these tails in the body of the weaving with a needle.

Once the weaving has a firm foundation, use other kinds of "yarns." Weave the next few rows by alternating one row of ribbon with one row of yarn, for example. You might put the ribbon in carefully so that it lies flat, or purposely crinkle and bend it. Weave right up to the notches on the bottom edge with any sort of material—yarn, cord, ribbon, twine, or leather.

Remove the collar from its cardboard pattern by sliding the warp threads off the notches. Weave the hanging tails into the wrong side of the piece with a needle, and trim them close after several stitches. Then sew three pieces of yarn 15″ long to each end of the neckline edge. Braid

these ends and tie them together to fasten the collar around your neck.

Make your next collar more involved by using other materials. For example, string large beads on the fill thread as you weave it into the warp. When you beat the rows into place toward the neckline edge, the beads will distribute themselves between each warp thread.

You might make the collar 8″ deep, instead of the 5″ you just used. Stop weaving 3″ or 4″ before you reach the bottom edge, and cut the warp threads open on that edge. Then slide a bead on each warp thread, and tie a knot to hold it in place. Your collar begins like a woven piece of fabric, but ends like a necklace.

After you have made some of the other projects in this book, apply their different weaves and materials to fashion a more unusual collar.

Fluffy Muff

Oriental carpets are made with a looping technique of *half hitches* that creates a fluffy surface. While you probably do not feel ready to tackle as large a project as a carpet, you can use the same technique to make a small but warm winter muff.

To make an improvised frame, cut two branches 21″ long. Cross them at the center so that the open ends of this "X" are 12″ wide, and lash the sticks together where they meet. Cut two more branches 12″ long and lash these to the open ends of the 21″-branches. With a penknife, make notches in the 12″-sticks, 12 notches to the inch.

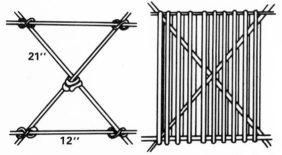

Illus. 3 (left). Four branches crossed and lashed to make a frame. Illus. 4 (right). Wrap warp around frame like this.

Wrap a strong cotton or linen warp around the 12″-sticks, placing one thread in each notch as you wind. The warp threads for a muff must surround the frame, not lie on top of it as for a collar (page 5). Since the muff is hollow, weave the warp threads on the front and back separately, and then slide the muff off the frame.

Collect heavy yarn in several shades of one color (for example, pink, red and maroon, which

Illus. 5. This muff uses the colors suggested on page 8. The half hitches were cut open to make the muff fluffy.

are all in the red family). For contrast, add a related shade that has a lot of another color in it (perhaps purple, which contains red, the original color, as well as a new color, blue).

To begin, weave four rows of purple in the tabby weave (over and under consecutive warp threads) on the front face of the frame. As soon as you weave a row, beat it to one end of the frame. Then with the next darkest color, maroon, make a row of loops:

First lay a ruler or other stick on top of the warp. With the fill thread, make *half hitches* in pairs facing each other, as shown in Illus. 6. Pull loops toward you as you make them up. Finish the entire row and remove the ruler. For thicker pile, make two or three rows of loops together, without separating them by any rows of tabby weaving. Begin the loops around the second warp in even rows to avoid weaving holes into the fabric. When you have completed the muff, decide whether or not to cut these loops open to have an even fluffier, more raised surface.

Weave three more rows of purple and loop another row of half hitches in red, the next darkest color. Weave another three rows of purple and again loop half hitches, in pink this time. Repeat this pattern. The gradations of color, from dark to light, make the pile appear deeper and richer than it actually is.

When you have woven across the front face of the frame, carefully pull a section of the unwoven warp around the end of the frame, so that it lies on top, and complete the weaving on this portion of the muff. Slide the woven muff off the frame.

For extra warmth, you should line the muff.

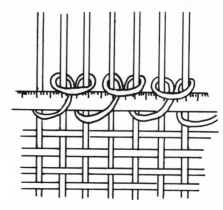

Illus. 6. Making half hitches by looping fill around a ruler.

Take a piece of lining fabric $1\frac{1}{2}''$ wider and $1\frac{1}{2}''$ longer than the muff itself and sew the ends together for a cylinder. Turn the lining so that its right side is out, and turn the muff so its wrong side is out. Slide the lining fabric over the wrong side of the muff. Sew the two pieces together by hand on the edges, turning the lining edge under at both selvages. Then turn the muff right side out and, with a combination of several of the yarns used for weaving, make a braid that is long enough to slip through the muff, hang around your neck, and balance the muff at about your waist. Thread this braid through the muff and tie the ends together in a square knot. Put your hands inside the muff and try it out on a brisk winter day!

To make a fluffy pillow, weave a muff as described above, but do not line it. Sew one end together and either stuff the pouch with scraps or insert a ready-made pillow. Toss pillows are

Illus. 7. To make a Persian Garden Carpet with a design in half hitches, weave several squares, each with a portion of the design. Sew the squares together to complete the carpet.

decorative, as well as soft and cuddly, when they are covered with pile.

You can even make a rug by sewing together small rectangles of woven pile. This would be a simple way to make a Persian Garden Carpet, composed of boxes filled with flowering plants. Pile of different colors alternated with flat areas of tabby weaving gives the impression of growing plants. The pile areas are the plants, and the flat background represents the surrounding earth.

Illus. 8. A multicolored rug using the pile technique described on page 8.

Doll

A woven doll makes a good companion for a little girl, as well as being a worthy member of a decorative doll collection. Use a square frame, described below, that allows you to weave sections of the warp independently from each other.

Use a square picture frame 12″ × 18″, a canvas stretcher that artists use, of the same dimensions, or make your own square frame by lashing four sticks together. The warp should be a stiff cotton thread; wrap it closely together around the 12″-sides of the frame, tying the beginning and end of the yarn to the edges of the frame. To hold the warp, you either insert nails on the 12″-edges of the frame, cut notches along those edges, or tape the warp threads as you wrap them.

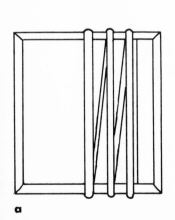

a   **b**

Illus. 9. In <u>a</u>, a square frame on which to weave a doll. In <u>b</u>, the side view, showing warp wrapped around frame.

Illus. 10. A doll with a peacock feather head has a body made by warp wrapping (see page 21). Colorful dolls also appear on the front cover.

11

When you weave fill, you use the warp threads on the front and back of the frame together, to get a flat piece, instead of weaving them separately for a cylinder as you did for your muff. The shape of the woven doll before you sew her together is like an upside-down tree: at the bottom of the frame, weave six "branches" by dividing the warp into six sections and using a different fill thread for each section.

Instead of weaving the fill threads parallel to the 12″-edge, pull them so they are on a 45° angle to the edge. Weave tightly enough so that each section is $\frac{3}{4}$″ wide. When the branches are 6″ long, weave the tails of all their fill threads in tabby across the warp for rows of fill which are parallel to the 12″-edge. Beat each row of this section into place. Weave this portion, which becomes the bodice of the doll, $4\frac{1}{4}$″ wide at the top and narrow it slightly to 4″ wide after a length of 2″.

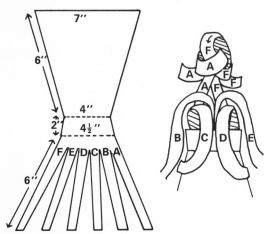

Illus. 11 (left). Diagram showing weaving pattern for doll. Illus. 12 (right). One way to assemble doll.

Continue weaving into the final 6″ of warp, and then weave more loosely so the warp fans out to a width of 7″. Weave right up to the end of the frame, cut the warp threads open, and remove the piece from the frame. Knot or sew the ends of the warp threads together.

The following description is only one way to attach the pieces to form the doll. Try this method first, and then experiment with your own ideas. Sew the sides of the skirt and bodice portions together to make a conical shape, stopping where the piece divides into sections. The seam you sew here is the doll's backbone.

Tuck the two middle branches, C and D, to the front and turn C to the left and D to the right. Then cross C and D in the back of the doll, and sew them to the doll's body where they cross. C and D form the shoulders of the doll.

Use branches B and E for the arms. Bend B over C, and sew them invisibly where they cross. Do the same with branches E and D. The ends of the arms dangle loosely at the doll's side, just as human arms would.

To make the neck, cross branches A and F, and make a few stitches where they meet. Then bring the two branches to the front, on opposite sides from where they begin, and cross them over each other. Take the ends of A and F behind the doll again. The crossing and recrossing of these branches makes a sturdy little head for the doll. Sew the ends of A and F to the doll as hair. If the texture of the weaving on the front of the head suggests facial features, accent these with other yarns or beads. Tie the ends of the arms with bits of yarn, to make wrists and hands.

You can weave dolls in many different shapes

Illus. 13. If you weave the warp on the front and back of the frame together, you can make a tubular doll like this.

and patterns. A doll made by "warp wrapping" groups of threads is shown in Illus. 10. This technique is described on page 21, in the instructions for the mobile.

Another idea you might try is to weave the front warp threads with one fill thread, then the back warp thread with the same fill, and then the front warp again. By alternating between the front and back warps, you will weave a tube. Weave the fill threads more tightly as you make your way up the warp, to make a cone that becomes the doll's skirt. At the top of the cone, weave the fill looser to form the bodice. For the separately formed head and arms, use three pieces of fill and make three smaller tubes. Begin the head piece very tightly, for the neck section, and then weave more loosely as you reach the head.

Scarf

From Peru to Pakistan, weaving on a *back strap* is an ancient method to hold the warp tight. The equipment is always available: you use your body to stretch the weaving as taut as it should be.

Place two nails in the floor or two pegs in the ground, 45″ apart, and wrap 40 warp threads around them, counting each 45″-length as one thread. Use soft yarns which are comfortable against your skin for the fill threads. You also need a needle with a large eye, a comb or fork to beat the fill, and a pair of scissors. Place a long wood dowel or stick through each end of the warp and remove the warp threads from the nails or pegs. Spread the warp threads evenly across the dowels and lay the dowels on a flat surface. Tape the threads to the dowels. With a belt or a piece of cord, tie one dowel to a stable object like a tree and the other dowel to your waist.

You can either sit or stand as you work, but stay far enough away from the solid support so that the warp is tense. Thread the needle with fill yarn and work it over and under alternate warp threads. Comb each row of fill toward you. Beat some fill strands tightly, others loosely, so that in

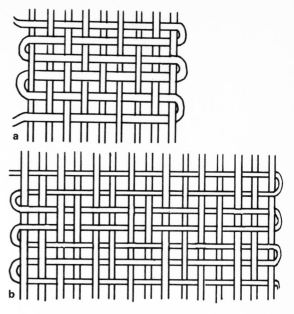

Illus. 15 a and b. Some variations of tabby.

one section warp dominates, in another fill does, and in another, there is a balance.

For more variety, make a pattern in the weaving by changing the number of warp threads the needle passes over and under. See Illus. 15 for some diagrams of different designs.

If you want to speed up your weaving, make a *harness* to raise and lower several warp threads at one time. This saves you the time-consuming task of separating the warp threads individually. Collect or buy four flat sticks 10″ long and 20 ice cream sticks. Drill a hole in the middle of each ice cream stick and place the sticks next to each other, $\frac{1}{8}$″ apart, so that each end of every ice cream stick

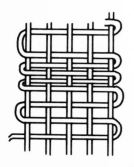

Illus. 14. Alternate weaving fill loosely and tightly for different effects.

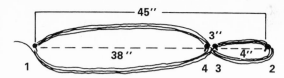

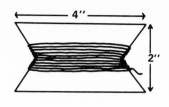

Illus. 16. If using a harness, wrap the warp around four pegs according to the dimensions shown here.

Illus. 18. Cardboard shuttle with fill wound on it.

lies on top of a 10"-stick. Glue the ice cream sticks in place there, and then glue the other two 10"-sticks on top of each end of the ice cream sticks. The ends of the ice cream sticks are thus sandwiched between the 10"-sticks.

If you use a harness, you must wrap the warp threads differently than before. Place two nails in the floor or pegs in the ground 45" apart, another peg 4" from one of them, and another 3" from the third. Wind a warp of 39 threads 50" long over the four pegs, so that the yarn crosses itself between the third and fourth pegs. With another strand of yarn, tie the warp threads securely at the cross. Place a dowel at the far end from the cross and

tie the end of the warp thread to this dowel. Insert another dowel where the second peg is. Remove the yarn from the pegs and cut the warp open at the end where the second peg was.

Now you are ready to *thread the harness*—that is, string the warp through the ice cream sticks. Untie the warp threads at the cross. Start with the first warp thread and insert it through the hole on the first stick. Put the second thread in the space between the first and second sticks. Continue in this manner, threading the odd threads through the holes and the even ones through the spaces between the sticks. Then tie pairs of warp together in square knots behind the heddle, and tape the warp threads evenly to the dowels. You have constructed a simple loom—but with no expense, no carpentry, and no special skills. Now you are ready to weave.

Wind fill yarn on a cardboard or wooden *shuttle*, a bobbin which carries the fill yarn and speeds your weaving. Unwind the yarn as you insert the shuttle over and under the warp threads. Using a shuttle is easier than the single thread: with the bulky shuttle wrapped with yarn, you can throw it through the warp quickly and easily.

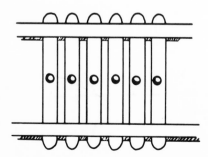

Illus. 17. Harness made of ice cream sticks.

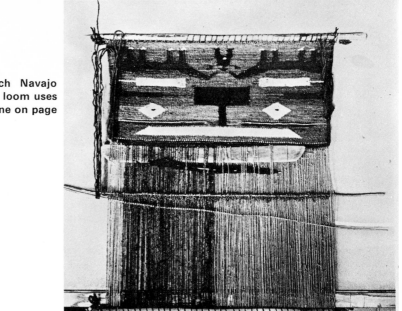

Illus. 19. A loom on which Navajo Indians weave blankets. This loom uses a string heddle bar like the one on page 17.

Tie yourself into the back strap with a cord or belt, as you did before (page 14). When you raise one end of the harness above the warp threads, the other end drops. While one end is raised, every other warp thread is also raised, and the alternate threads are lowered. The space between the warp threads is called the *shed*, and by opening a shed you can pass the fill, wrapped around the shuttle, through all the warp threads in a single motion. Leave a few inches of the fill thread hanging at the beginning corner of your scarf.

Beat the first row of fill toward you. Now change the position of the warp threads by reversing the harness: lower the end that was raised, and raise the end that was lowered. You have created a new shed, and the warp threads are opposite to the position they were just in. Weave the complete warp, changing the position of the harness after every row, and rewinding the shuttle when it runs out of fill. In almost no time at all, you can complete a handwoven piece of cloth—in a color and design that you have chosen.

Weaving of patterns more complicated than tabby is not necessarily more difficult: re-thread the harness so that you skip either some holes or spaces. When you raise one end, then, several adjacent threads will be raised. You can also raise warp threads by hand with a pointed stick.

For extra softness, loop some rows of pile into the scarf as you weave the fill thread. See page 8.

Poncho and Tunic

You can make even ponchos, tunics or dresses without a loom if you make your garment of separately woven pieces. You will need a frame on which to weave, about 21″ × 31″. To make notches for the warp threads, hammer nails $\frac{1}{8}$″ apart on the frame's 21″-sides, or else saw $\frac{1}{4}$″-deep slits $\frac{1}{8}$″ apart on the shorter sides. You can also use the frame without any notches, but you must then position the warp carefully as you wind.

Choose a warp which is stronger than the fill. To make a rich color and texture, combine several different threads for the warp or fill. One attractive method is to use several related colors and one unrelated, for contrast. The color wheel in Illus. 20 should help you make your color choices. Because adjacent colors are related to each other they blend harmoniously. Colors opposite each other are strong contrasts and form striking combinations.

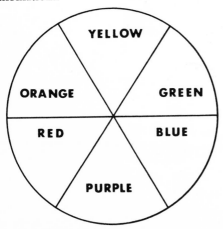

Illus. 20. Color wheel.

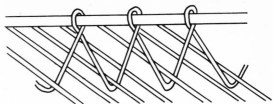

Illus. 21. String heddle bar attached to every other warp thread.

Tie one end of the warp yarn to the corner of the frame, or around a corner nail or slit. If you hammered nails or sawed slits as instructed above, they are $\frac{1}{8}$″ apart, and the warp threads you wrap around the frame are also $\frac{1}{8}$″ apart. If you are not using nails or slits, wrap and tape warp threads $\frac{1}{8}$″ apart. Surround the frame with warp and then end the warp the same way you began it.

You used an ice cream stick harness when you wove the scarf (page 14); for the poncho, a string heddle bar also raises threads while allowing a greater flexibility of design. Find a smooth stick or dowel 23″ long, or slightly longer than the narrow edge of the frame. Loop a strong string in half hitches (see page 8) alternately between the dowel and every other warp thread. (You weave the warp threads together which are wound on the front and back of the frame, so you might attach those threads on the back to the string heddle bar.) You can use other arrangements for different weaves, of course. Place this bar toward the top of the frame. When you lift the string heddle bar, the warp threads which are connected to it also rise.

Find a flat, smooth stick approximately 2″ × $\frac{1}{4}$″ × 23″ to slide over every warp thread connected to the string heddle bar, and under

Illus. 22. A tunic made of woven cloth. Instructions for assembling the tunic are on page 20.

every one not connected. When you turn the stick so its $\frac{1}{4}''$-side is against the warp, the threads that it lies under are raised, while the threads below it are lowered. Position this *sword* toward the back of the frame, at the opposite end from the string heddle bar. By alternately raising the string heddle bar and the sword, you make opposite sheds to weave into.

Make a simple cardboard shuttle (see page 15) and wrap fill around it. Raise the string heddle bar and throw the shuttle through the shed. Beat this first row of fill to the end of the frame with

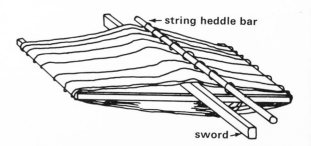

Illus. 23. Weave by alternately turning the sword and pulling the string heddle bar.

18

a comb. Then turn the sword on its side so it raises those warp threads which were lowered in the first shed, and pass the shuttle through this shed. Repeat this pattern, changing sheds and throwing fill. Change the fill yarn—either randomly or regularly—to vary the color and texture of your work.

When you are weaving the second shed (that is, when the sword is turned so it raises some threads), release the heddle bar so it does not raise the other threads—but do not release it so much that the thread connecting it to the warp becomes woven into your cloth.

Weave right up to the ends of the frame, and then cut the front and back warp threads apart so you can remove the cloth. Knot the warp threads together in small groups of two or three threads and finish off these ends by threading them back into the weaving.

To construct the poncho, weave another piece of cloth the same size and color as the first. Sew the two pieces together with yarn by curving and stitching them as shown in Illus. 24. A poncho of this size fits an average woman.

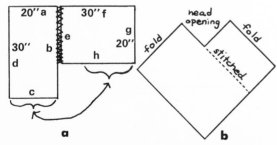

Illus. 24. Sew the poncho together as shown in view **a**. View **b** shows the completed poncho.

Illus. 25. Another article of clothing made by off-loom weaving. This is a scarf made by *sprang*. See page 33.

19

You can make a tunic by following the weaving instructions for a poncho, with one addition: add a different color and stronger fill thread after every 3" of weaving. For each of these threads, leave a tail about 4" long hanging from one selvage. Weave four pieces, two more than for the poncho. Each piece will be 20" × 30".

Place two of these pieces on a flat surface with the 30"-edges touching. The threads from the fill yarn should hang from those 30"-edges which do not touch. Sew the two woven pieces together for 21" with a piece of yarn going back and forth between them. Do the same with the other two woven pieces. Place the four pieces together so the unstitched sections meet in the middle. This opening is for your head. Sew the seams on each side of the opening as you sewed the others.

Now that you have sewn the tunic pieces together, fit the tunic to your body. Gather the weaving by pulling the fill tails which are below the neck opening on both the front and back of the tunic, until the width of the entire piece equals the width of your shoulders. Tie a knot in each tail at the selvage to keep the gathering in place. Leave the fabric across your shoulders the full width for small sleeves. Weave the tails from the fill threads which you did not gather into the body

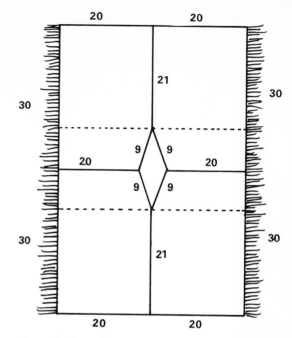

Illus. 26. Sew four woven pieces together like this for the tunic in Illus. 22.

of the tunic. Leave the gathering threads hanging decoratively, or tie them together to join the front and back of the tunic.

Mobile Using Warp Wrapping

A mobile makes a decorative ornament to spruce up a bare wall or hang above a baby's crib. A woven mobile is particularly good for babies, as it is soft and safe. The technique of *warp wrapping* is used for the mobile shown in Illus. 31.

Loop about 50 half hitches on a ruler or other rigid stick, for 50 cords that are each 1 yard long. Tape the ruler to a solid support like a window ledge—something which is immovable, but which protrudes from the wall so there is working space all around. Tie the ends of the strands in pairs through curtain weights (found in a sewing notions shop). Weighting the warp threads with heavy objects makes weaving easier, because you can work with the free hanging warp without worrying about knotting at the ends of the threads.

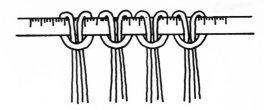

Illus. 27. Make 50 half hitches on a ruler.

Divide the warp into eight or ten groups with the same number of threads in each group. Use a needle to weave two rows of tabby in one group of warp, so the fill is caught in it. Tightly holding that group of warp toward you, simply wrap the fill thread around and around the warp threads. If you do not twist the warp yarns, the wrapped fill threads will not undo when you release the tension of the warp.

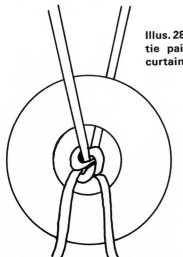

Illus. 28. To weight the cords, tie pairs of warp through curtain weights.

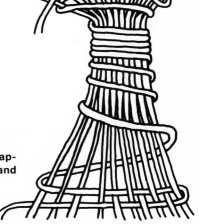

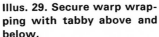

Illus. 29. Secure warp wrapping with tabby above and below.

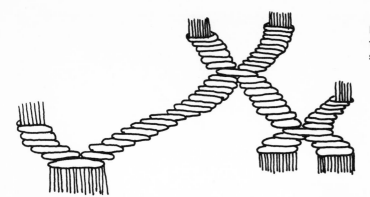

Illus. 30. Group wrapped warp threads together and wrap a few times. Then separate again.

After working on one group of warp for a distance, weave a temporary row of tabby to hold your weaving in place and move on to another warp section. Repeat the procedure with the groups of warp across the ruler. Regroup the warp threads and wrap them also, so that every part of the mobile is connected to every other part. The wrapped groups should come together and separate throughout the piece to hold it together.

As the weaving takes shape, plan how you would like the rest of the mobile to fall. Join the strips of warp wrapping so that the air catches and blows them at random. The mobile pictured here combines the tabby weave with warp wrapping, but you may use any weaving technique you wish.

When all the warp has been wrapped and woven, you may leave it on the stick from which it hung, or substitute a flexible reed. The mobile in Illus. 31 hangs from hooks on the ceiling, but you may prefer to fasten your mobile to the wall. Whichever you choose, secure the wrapped sections away from each other, so they do not just hang limply.

Illus. 31. A mobile using tabby weave and warp wrapping softly moves when the least breeze blows.

22

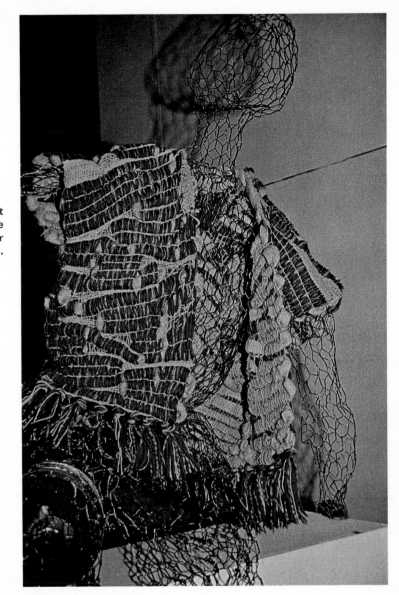

Illus. 32. Vest uses colors that are opposites to emphasize undulating fill. See page 31 for instructions for undulating fill.

Spinning

While weaving usually uses store-bought wool, you might enjoy spinning your own wool for a change. You can then completely make a garment yourself—from spinning the wool to weaving it into cloth to sewing it into clothing. Spinning is not difficult, and the nubby threads which frequently result offer a refreshing and attractive contrast to the perfectly spun wool you buy.

Nomadic shepherds made spindles by setting a wooden dowel into a clay or stone whorl, the round piece which balances the dowel as it spins. For your whorl, cut a potato slice or a piece of plastic foam (called Styrofoam in the United States) 3″ in diameter by $\frac{3}{4}$″ thick. Insert a wooden dowel $\frac{3}{8}$″ thick × 18″ long through the center of the circle. Attach the dowel to the slice by first tying a string to the dowel a few inches above the whorl; then pass the string below the whorl and around the dowel a few times. Bring the string

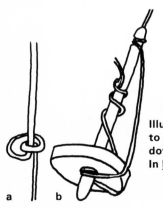

Illus. 33. In a, the knot to attach the wooden dowel to the whorl. In b, the spindle.

a   b

24

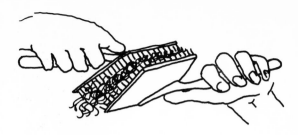

Illus. 34. "Teasing" wool with dog brushes.

back to the top of the dowel, and tie a half hitch in a notch $\frac{3}{4}$″ from the tip of the dowel.

Now that your spindle is ready to accept spun wool, you must also prepare the wool. You can buy unspun wool at craft shops, or direct from ranches which raise sheep. The customary way to comb the fibres is to *tease* the wool with several branches of dried "teasel," a prickly herb which grows in the marshlands. You can use two wire dog brushes if you cannot find teasel. Place a small tuft of wool between the dog brushes and pull them apart three or four times. The natural oils in the wool make the fibres stick to each other while you loosely roll the wool together in one long rope, called the *roving*.

Now you are ready to spin the wool into one long even thread. Hold the spindle in one hand and throw the roving over your other arm. Moisten the end of the roving slightly and twist the string which you wrapped on the spindle into the damp wool. With your other hand, carefully stretch the combed fibres apart to thin them. Keep your upper hand in place but release the pressure of your other hand on the string. As the spindle twists, it carries the twist into the fibres of

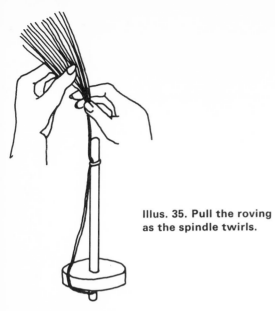

Illus. 35. Pull the roving as the spindle twirls.

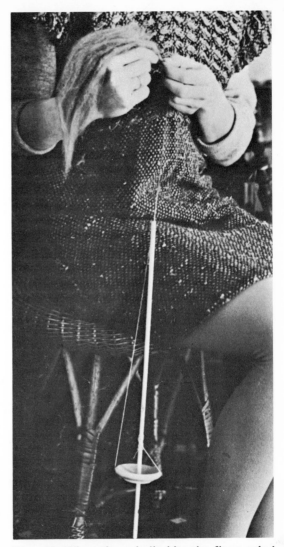

Illus. 36. When the spindle hits the floor, wind the spun wool around the wooden dowel. Then spin again.

the wool and pulls the wool into one thin thread. Grasp the spun wool an inch or so below the beginning of the roving while you twirl the spindle with the other hand, and move up the roving with your hand as you spin more and more thread.

When the spun yarn is so long that the spindle hits the floor, stop spinning. Unhook the string which you attached at the notch and wrap it around the dowel, also wrapping the attached spun yarn. Leave enough yarn unwrapped to grasp above the notch so you can continue to spin.

When the spindle is full, cut the spun yarn from the roving and loosely wind it into a ball. Tie another string to the spindle and make a second length. If this is your first work, the yarn will probably have an uneven, homespun texture and be kinky because you have spun too tightly. As you practice spinning, you will gain control of the yarn's thickness. Wrap the yarn on a *niddy noddy* (see Illus. 37) to unkink it slowly, or, if you are in a hurry, wash and dry the yarn and hang it from a weighted rod. Always wash your spun wool so it shrinks before you weave it.

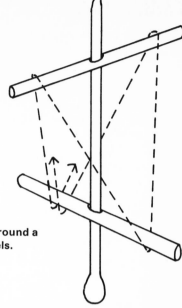

Illus. 37. To straighten the wool, wrap it around a *niddy noddy* made from wooden dowels.

Indian Belt

You can weave a belt simply and quickly with a simple technique that uses the warp threads as both warp and fill. An ordinary braid, made with three strands, is an example of this; because the warp threads are secured only at one end, they can cross over each other to make a strip of weaving as tight or loose as you wish, with no fill threads to beat.

Just as you did for the mobile (page 21), loop 48 half hitches on a ruler so that each of the 48 hanging cords is 2 yards long. Tape the ruler on which you mounted the cords to a sturdy support around waist-level (again, a window ledge is ideal) and sit facing it.

Begin by weaving the warp thread on the far left in tabby through the other strands, over one and under one, until you reach the middle of the warp. Then weave the warp thread on the far right toward the left. When these two threads meet in the middle, cross them over each other so they change sides, and drop them. Pick up what are now the outer threads and weave them toward

Illus. 39. This Indian belt was made by the Pawnee Indians in Oklahoma. The zigzag design arose in southeast Canada and later spread widely through the eastern United States.

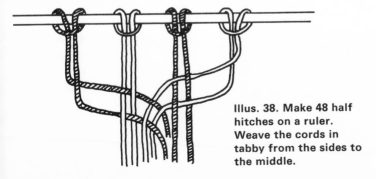

Illus. 38. Make 48 half hitches on a ruler. Weave the cords in tabby from the sides to the middle.

the center as you did with the first pair. Weave through the first two threads which are now in the center, and cross them also. Weave in this fashion until $\frac{1}{2}''$ from the end of the warp. Knot every two warp threads together and leave this fringe as a decorative edge. Slip the half hitches off the ruler at the beginning of the belt and tie a short fringe on each loop by this method: slip three or four pieces of yarn, each 8″ long, halfway through one loop. Wrap one end of one strand around the others several times and then draw the end through the wrappings. Pull tightly and the fringe will not undo.

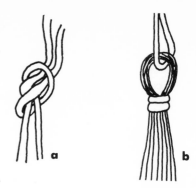

Illus. 40. In a, the way to secure the woven cords' ends. In b, fringe added to top loops.

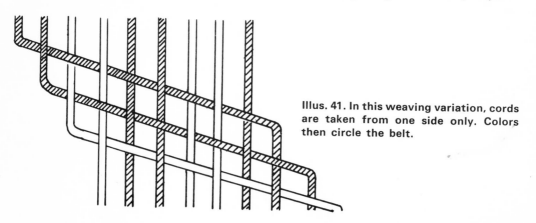

Illus. 41. In this weaving variation, cords are taken from one side only. Colors then circle the belt.

To make a slightly different belt, try this method of using warp as fill: instead of weaving with yarn from both sides, take it from the same side every time, and weave across all the warp threads. If you use different colors for the warp, the colors will look as if they are travelling around the belt in a circle.

Another variation is to weave in any pattern for several inches and then divide the warp into several groups. Weave these groups separately along most of the length of the belt; then bring the groups together and weave all the warp threads together again.

Woven Picture

Before printing was invented, a frequent way of telling a story was to represent it visually, frequently in colorful tapestries. Artists today sometimes have their paintings executed in tapestry form. Because weaving is flat, it is a logical medium to use for portraying simple drawings. Even if you are not an artist, you can weave a beautiful tapestry by using simple shapes and attractive shades that harmonize well. The design you choose should be plain: an uncomplicated pattern

Illus. 42. A woven face, with different weaves showing different planes of the face.

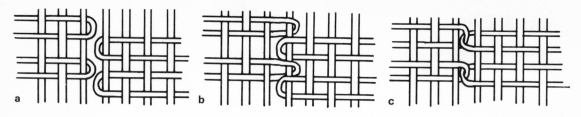

Illus. 43. Ways to join adjacent sections of fill: in <u>a</u>, weaving fill up to the same warp thread. In <u>b</u>, weaving fill around the same warp thread. In <u>c</u>, weaving one strand of fill around another.

with large areas of solid colors is a good one for a beginning weaver.

Find or make a frame that is either the same size or slightly larger than the picture you are using. Choose a warp of tightly spun linen or cotton yarn in a neutral color and wrap warp threads $\frac{1}{4}''$ apart around the frame, over nails, slots or the frame itself. After wrapping the warp threads, tape your drawing to the back of the frame and collect yarns that are as close to its colors as possible. If you cannot find the exact colors you want, you may be able to simulate the right shade by combining different colors together: from a distance, for example, red and blue yarns look purple. The color combinations you achieve depend, however, on the shades that you begin with: orange-red and blue-green make brown, not purple. You should experiment to make sure that the individual shades produce the final color you want.

After you have taped the picture to be copied to the back of the frame—or, if the picture is smaller than the frame, to another piece of paper which you tape to the frame—weave several rows

of tabby with the fill yarn across the base of the picture to support the rest of the weaving. When you finish the piece, you can either turn this section under and hem it, or pull it out.

With the picture taped to the back of the frame, you can see at a glance what color yarns to weave. Because the picture and therefore the frame are probably not too large, the warp threads do not allow enough space for a shuttle to weave the fill threads. It is easiest to thread a large-eyed needle with fill and weave over and under the warp threads—on the front and back of the frame together—with the needle. When you reach the end of one section of color, there are three ways to join the section with the next, as shown in Illus. 43.

Make every shape in your weaving the same shape it is in the picture. Beat the fill toward the frame's base as you weave. After you have completed the picture, weave several rows of fill across the top of the warp as you did at the beginning. You might weave bamboo sticks or other light reeds at the top and bottom to maintain the tapestry's shape.

Lamp Shade

A handwoven lamp shade is much more color-ful than the somber monotone shades found in department stores. Because you can weave on anything that stretches the warp taut, a curved lamp shade makes as good a frame for weaving as a flat frame does.

Buy or make a lamp shade base with stiff wire, or cut the fabric off an old lamp shade. Choose a natural yarn such as wool or cotton (synthetic yarns burn easily) and string a warp of a neutral color around the top and bottom of the shade. Tape the warp to the frame. For other projects you have taken care to space the warp threads evenly: for a lamp shade, space them irregularly instead. While woven threads are usually arranged in straight horizontal and vertical rows, it is interesting to vary this placement sometimes. Warp does not have to be uniformly spaced, nor does fill have to travel evenly over and under the warp. In making your lamp shade, you can form *undulating fill*, which makes waves up and down, to match the circular form of the shade.

First, decide upon the pattern and colors you wish to use. One attractive arrangement is to choose your colors to connote different aspects of nature: use greens and browns to represent the earth, blue for sky or water, and bright yellow for the sun. Purple is a mysterious color which adds shadows and rich tones to your weaving. Incorporate it into your design, for its presence is sure to be felt.

Look at the warp you have threaded and imagine a line about three-fourths of the way up the shade's base. Below that line, weave colors to show the earth, and above it, weave colors for the sky. The line should undulate, or wander and wave, as it moves around trees (which you will weave in green and brown), brooks (deep blue), and mountains (white, for snowy caps).

Make three straight lines of fill at the base of the frame to give the rest of your weaving a firm foundation. Using either the same color or a similar one, to continue the feeling of earth, weave a small patch which becomes narrower at the top. Weave another triangle nearby, and then loosely weave a third color around and between the two triangles. This is the fill which "undulates" or waves with the colors. Weave the next fill thread in so it loosely curves over the solid shapes, and then use the color to add more shaped pieces. When you weave different colors next to each other, lock them together as you did for the woven picture (page 29).

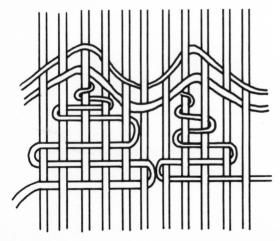

Illus. 44. Undulating fill wanders up and down the warp, while small triangles of fill cover warp.

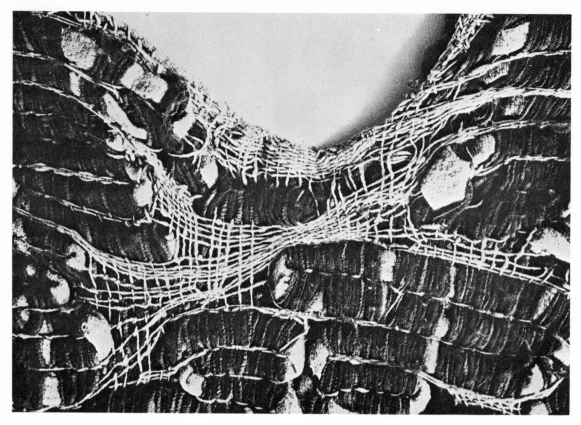

Illus. 45. Close-up of undulating fill on the neckline of a vest.

Weave small portions of the landscape at a time, but remember that you are working on a round frame. Keep working around the shade so you weave similarly all round. The weaving should gradually evolve in both shape and color to the horizon line, and then the colors should switch from earthy tones to those of the sky. The sudden contrast in color is softened by the gentle waving line.

Baby Carrier

While most of the projects until now have been decorative, you can also weave something practical. With a baby carrier over one shoulder and on your opposite side, you can watch the baby as you perform your chores. The technique used for making the carrier involves a twisting pattern related to weaving called *sprang*. Wooden dowels hold the twisted warp threads which are wrapped around each other, rather than around fill threads. As more warp threads are twisted, you remove the dowels. The finished piece is loose and lacy, similar to the woven hammocks that are strung between trees.

Set a frame 18" × 26" on a flat surface. Gather six wooden dowels, each 18" long, and sharpen four of them at both ends. Place the two dowels which are not sharpened on one side of the frame, each one 6" from an 18"-side, and tape the dowels to the outside of the frame. Crisscross a rope between the dowels, and leave a long tail hanging from the knot holding the twine to the dowel.

Choose a smooth, sturdy yarn such as cotton twine, found in hardware stores. Tie the end of the twine to the end of one of the dowels on the frame, and wrap the twine away from the other dowel, around the front of the frame, and to the second dowel. Loop it around this dowel and then carry it to the front of the frame again and to the first dowel. Continue wrapping warp, about 4 threads per inch, across the entire frame. Tie the end of the twine to a dowel temporarily, while you pull all the threads to an even, flexible tension, and then tie the twine securely to the dowel.

Turn the frame over so the dowels are on the

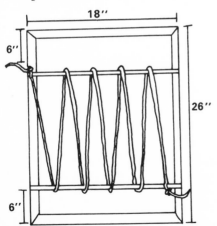

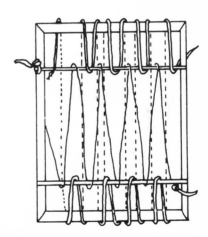

Illus. 46 (left). As you twist *sprang*, the warp becomes very tight. Attach dowels to back of frame so they, and thus the warp, can be loosened. Illus. 47 (right). Wrap warp loosely around the dowels on the back of the frame.

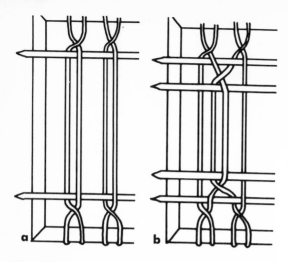

Illus. 48. In **a**, the warp has been twisted once. In **b**, warp has been regrouped and twisted.

twisting results in two twists, one at each end of the frame.

On the next row, skip the first warp thread and twist the second and third threads together. Insert two more dowels and push them toward the ends, as you did in the first row. After you have twisted the second row, check the first one for mistakes; you can easily see them after you twist the next row. If there is a mistake, pull the dowels out just up to the incorrect pair of threads, and retwist from that point.

When you have completed two rows of twisting, pull out the first two dowels and regroup the pairs of warp as they were for the first row. Continue by alternating the pairs you used in the first and second rows. Twisting tightens the warp threads, so you must loosen the dowels at the back of the frame occasionally: untie the twine holding them together and slide the dowels closer to the edges of the frame. When the two sections of twisting almost meet in the middle, finish the piece: using a crochet hook (or your fingers, if the

bottom and place the frame in your lap. Now you are ready to begin twisting the warp yarns to form the lacy pattern. Begin at the same side for every row, and use the hand that is on the same side as the direction toward which you are twisting. For example, the right hand should twist if you are moving from left to right. Use your two first fingers to twist the first two threads around each other. Insert one of the pointed dowels into the opening which is formed between these two threads, and continue twisting pairs across the warp, inserting the dowel in the openings as you progress. When you reach the end of the row, pull the dowel toward you to the end of the frame. Insert another dowel in the same shed and push it to the other end of the frame. Thus, one row of

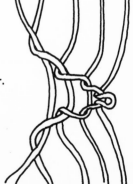

Illus. 49. To finish sprang weaving, make a chain of loops down the center. Tie the last two loops together.

Illus. 50. The sprang technique is often used in hammocks made of rope. This is a close-up of a sprang hammock.

warp isn't too tight), make a chain with the remaining warp. To start the chain, pull the second warp thread under and over the first. Pull the third thread through the loop of the second, the fourth through the third, and continue in this way across the warp. Tie the last two chain links together with a short piece of twine and remove the remaining two dowels.

Turn the frame over so the two dowels laced together face up. Unlace the dowels from each other and tie the warp temporarily to the dowels with yarn. Then remove the sprang from the frame.

To make the shoulder strap, fold two 6-yard pieces of twine in half and pass the loop formed at the fold through one of the links in the carrier.

Illus. 51. Make a shoulder strap for the baby carrier with the chain stitch.

Reach into this loop from above and grasp the shoulder strap yarn, pulling it through the first loop to make another loop. Repeat this chain stitch until the strap is long enough to go over your head and hold the baby slightly above your waist. Tie the strap securely to the other side of the sprang.

Use this twisting pattern with a softer and finer yarn—knitting worsted or soft ribbon—to make a long scarf. Attach three or four sprang sections together at the looped ends with the chain stitch. See page 19 for a sprang scarf in color.

For a large hammock, twist strong yarn into at least 12 sprang pieces and join them with the chain stitch as you did for a sprang scarf.

Try twisting in different patterns. You might use several warp threads together as one, or twist pairs that turn in opposite directions.

Indian Wampum Necklace

Illus. 52. A wampum collar used on formal occasions by Indian tribes of northeastern United States. It is made of clam and conch shells.

American Indians traded strings of beads, nuts and berries called *wampum* and used them as money. Bows served as their frames for weaving, because the curve of a bow has just enough spring in it to hold the warp taut, while adjusting to any changes in tension.

You can copy the Indians' weaving technique to make a necklace by using a toy bow from a child's bow and arrow set, or a sturdy yet flexible branch. If you use a bow, remove the string that is used for shooting arrows. Buy two $2\frac{1}{2}''$-metal springs at a hardware store and tie one to each end of the bow or branch. Collect dried berries or beads to weave in your necklace, and plan the arrangement of colors on graph paper before you begin.

Once you have determined the pattern you wish to weave, wrap a continuous linen warp around the two springs, letting the threads of the warp slip into the spirals of the spring to hold them in place. Space the threads according to the size of your beads, but allow enough room between each thread for at least one bead. Weave the front and back warp separately, as you did for the fluffy muff (page 7), to make a circular necklace that will not need fasteners or clasps.

For the colorful beads to stand out, use the same yarn for fill that you did for warp. Thread a needle with this yarn and slip the number of beads on the needle that are to lie between the first and second threads. Loop the fill thread in a half hitch around the first warp thread, position the beads properly, and loop the thread around the second warp thread. Slide the next bead or group of beads on the fill thread, and continue to the end of the row. Carefully comb this row into place at one end of the frame, and, using the same fill thread, reverse your direction for the next row.

To make the weaving go faster, you might equip your loom with a string heddle bar and sword (page 17). When you open a shed, you can slide the whole row of beads between the warp

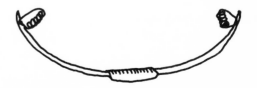

Illus. 53. Remove the string from a child's bow and attach two springs to the ends.

37

threads. Carefully comb the beads into their proper positions. While this method of construction is not as sturdy as looping the fill in half hitches around the warp with a needle, its ease and speed make it a practical way to weave.

Move the unwoven warp to the top of the frame as you need it, so that you weave all portions. If the warp is taped to the springs, retape it each time you move the warp.

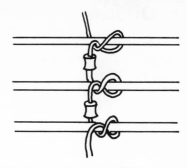

Illus. 54. String beads on the fill thread and wrap it around the warp in half hitches.

Room Divider

For a porch, playroom or studio where you want a natural feeling inside, make a woven screen out of natural materials. Take a country walk during late autumn, when you can see the shapes of branches of different trees. Choose those you like, and mix them with sturdy twisting vines like grape or bittersweet. If your walk can only be a city one, go to a florist for dried rushes, wheat and seed pods.

Choose a strong and natural yarn like linen for the warp. This lasts longer than jute, its rough cousin. Use natural colors or clear plastic fishing line for the warp, so that it disappears in the light and gives the impression that the fill branches are climbing by themselves.

Buy two curtain rods of the width that you want the finished divider to be. Hang one from hooks screwed into the ceiling where the divider will hang permanently, and slip the other rod through screw eyes placed in the floor directly beneath the first rod. Wrap a continuous warp around the two rods and use the threads on the front and back together as one warp. Collect other materials for fill such as ribbon, scrap leather, and feathers.

Thread a needle with the yarn you used for the warp and weave several rows as fill at the base of the divider, for a support upon which to work. Then spread the branches for fill on the floor and see if they have any design characteristics, such as a curve that can be accented by placing several similarly curved pieces together. Weave the branches over and under the warp with your fingers. To lock the fill in place, use a variation of

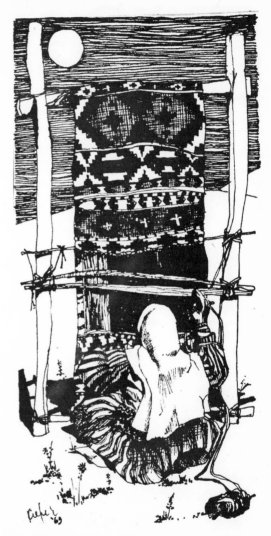

Illus. 55. An artist's sketch of a large frame on which to weave. A woven piece this big might be used for a room divider.

Illus. 56. Detail of a room divider woven with natural materials. Ferns, cattails, and moss as well as other plants were used.

the sprang technique (page 33) called *leno*. In leno, warp threads are twisted as they are in sprang, but instead of passing a temporary dowel through the warp threads, you pass a fill yarn which remains permanently. The pairs of warp threads which twist are always the same two threads, so untwisted warp threads never lie on the outside of alternate rows as they do in sprang.

Apply any methods of weaving you have practiced to your room divider. Combine leno with a fill of softly beaten yarn between branches which need a regular support. Add small areas of pile (see page 8) to change the texture occasionally, and insert sections of warp wrapping (page 21) when it seems appropriate. Beads and natural berries, which you used for your Indian wampum necklace (page 37), should blend perfectly with

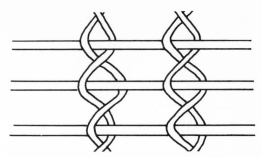

Illus. 57. In leno twisting, the same two warp threads are twisted around each other. A fill thread keeps them from untwisting.

the other natural materials you are using here. Your creativity in using the weaving techniques you already know determines your ability in this craft.

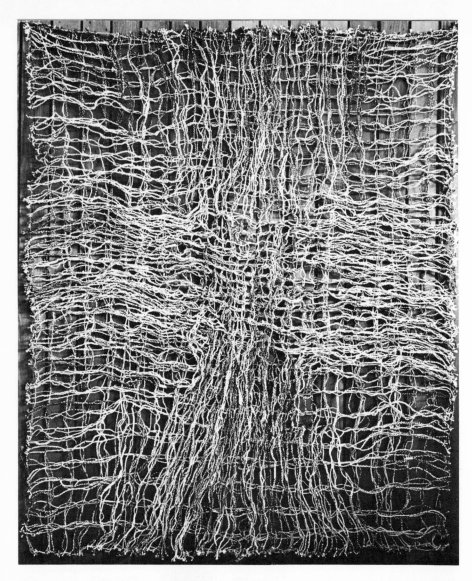

Illus. 58. A wall hanging of synthetic raffia which has been knotted and braided.

Indian Feather Cape

American Indians are familiar with a practical piece of clothing, the feather cape. California Indians use it as a ceremonial dance costume, while in South America its naturally greased feathers provide protection against the rain. The cape is knotted in a loose pattern called "fisherman's knots," and then feathers are wrapped around the cords. The charm of this delicate piece, as well as its simple construction, should inspire you to make it.

Using a natural yarn like jute or sisal (synthetic yarns slip and so do not hold the knots), hold the cord a few inches from the end and make the knot diagrammed in Illus. 59. Hook this loop to a nail, doorknob, or even your big toe, and turn the loop so the knot is on either side of the nail.

Grasping the loop with your first two fingers in the middle, insert the end of the yarn through the loop from the top to the bottom. (You might find it convenient to wind the long cord into a ball for easier handling.) Keep your little finger in the new loop (formed as you pull the end of the yarn) to hold it about 6″ long. Now pinch the first loop just above the point where the second passes through it, and pass the end of the yarn under the first loop, around and over it. Insert the end of the yarn between the cord and the first loop, and pull it tight. See Illus. 60 for the visual instructions.

Grasp the second loop in the middle so the knots on each end of the loop are together. Form a third knot as you did the second. Continue in this

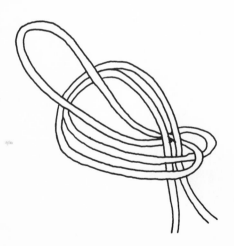

Illus. 59. To start an Indian feather cape, make this knot.

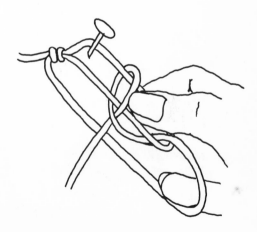

Illus. 60. Grasp the first knot with your thumb and index finger and make a second loop.

Illus. 61. An Indian feather cape, viewed from the inside. The feathers hang in even rows and offer protection against rain.

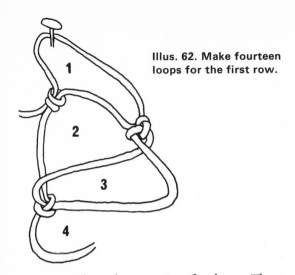

Illus. 62. Make fourteen loops for the first row.

manner until you have a series of 14 knots. These knots zigzag down the row, one formed to the right side, the next to the left.

To make the second row, insert the yarn midway into the 13th loop, from the right side if you are right-handed, from the left if you are left-handed. Knot a new loop by grasping one side of the 13th loop, and then work up the row, making new loops in each loop of the first row. When you reach the end of Row 2, start down for Row 3, looping into the end loop of Row 2 to begin.

Make at least 10 rows of knots and loops, for a base about 18″ × 21″. With two half hitches, hook a piece of yarn 1½ yards long to one corner of the base along the side where there are 10 rows. Make a tie with the chain stitch. Do the same at the other corner 10 loops away. When you wear the cape, drape it over your shoulders and tie it in front.

Collect 60 feathers about 10″ long wherever you can get them—from a farmer or a poultry market—or purchase natural colored feathers in a toy or craft shop. Soak the feathers in warm water overnight so the quills are flexible. Beginning with the bottom row of loops, fold a quill over the cord midway between two knots, and tuck the tip of the quill into the hollow stem of the feather. You may have to prick the stem open with a pin. If you are using smaller feathers that have narrow stems, bend the quills over the cord and fold them against the feather's stem. Wrap the quills with a strong, thin thread to hold them around the cord.

Attach feathers on each loop of the bottom row. Skip the second row and hook feathers to the third row. Skip alternate rows over the entire net. When you are finished, the knotted base is cloaked in feathers, providing protection as well as fashion.

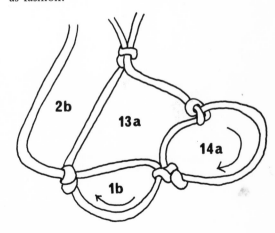

Illus. 63. Begin the second row by making a loop through the thirteenth one of the first row.

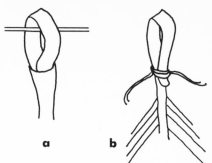

Illus. 65. In <u>a</u>, quill is looped over cord and tip inserted into hollow stem. In <u>b</u>, stem is too narrow, so thread wraps around tip and stem.

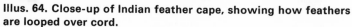

Illus. 64. Close-up of Indian feather cape, showing how feathers are looped over cord.

Summary

By making these projects, you have learned that interlacing horizontal threads into vertical threads is called weaving. The running stitch of sewing is the simplest form of weaving, as it is simply interlacing a thread into cloth.

Man's first weaving probably developed by looking at nature. In the animal kingdom there are birds called weaverbirds who weave nests; beavers weave dams and the spider weaves his homespun web. Plants weave, too: grape vines interlace themselves for support, and woven palm tree fronds grow with flexible support that allows them to do without branches.

Our early weaving used the same materials that nature uses. Early weaving was practical: baskets to carry food, and mats on which to sleep. Mats were made larger to become roof tops and house sides that were light and portable. Man also wore these woven mats: Indians of the American Northwest wove rain hats and capes with flexible grasses and the softened inner bark of cedar trees. But this clothing must have rubbed the skin, so when the rains stopped the itchy victim probably searched for a soft material he could weave into an undergarment. Perhaps the Indian found wool caught in pasture briars from roaming herds and was intrigued by its softness. Since he already spun rope from short strands of vines by twisting them together against his thigh, he applied that technique to the short woollen fibres and soon had long strands of yarn with which to weave soft clothing.

But this flexible yarn also presented a problem. While rigid materials hold their place and therefore can easily be woven, yarns blow around and need support. So the Indian experimented with different solutions. He hung the strands, weighted them from a branch, stretched them between a tree trunk and his back, or wrapped them around two rigid bars. Then the weaver worked a horizontal fill into the vertical warp. But this was still thinking in sewing terms, a time-consuming approach. Devising a way to raise many warp threads at a time led to the development of the loom. The term "loom" generally refers to a machine at which the weaver sits, with the warp at table height. But long ago the Indians, and now you, have found that satisfying and useful woven articles can be made without the complications and expense of a loom.

Index